Internet Business Success Formula

Only Way Left for Little Guy to Make a Killing Online

By Meir Liraz

Published by BizMove
www.bizmove.com

Copyright © Liraz Publishing. All rights reserved.

ISBN: 9781696952316

Table of Contents

1. The Single Most Critical Factor in Making Money with an Internet Business	5
2. Internet Business Beginners Tips and Ideas	10
3. Locating Profit-Driving Keywords	34
4. Creating a Stream of income	39
5. Creating a Money Making Website	45
6. Effective Link Building Strategies	53
Appendix 1: The 50 Best Paying Affiliate Marketing Markets	66
Appendix 2: Sources for Backlinks Sorted by Category and Page Rank	69

MEIR LIRAZ

INTERNET BUSINESS SUCCESS FORMULA

1. The Single Most Critical Factor in Making Money with an Internet Business

There is a special breed of Online-Millionaires that are making money on the internet like crazy. You've probably never heard of them. They keep themselves and their activities under the radar. Why? because they follow a certain simple strategy and they don't want you or anyone else to discover it. This strategy has created more millionaires than you could ever think possible.

How do I know? I am one of those Millionaires, and I'm going to reveal to you now each and every component of this incredible strategy.

My name is Meir Liraz. You may have stumbled on my name on the internet, probably in relation to my capacity as a writer and publisher of business guides. This is just one side of me, the visible one. There has been another side to my online presence, a concealed one. And there is where I've been taking advantage of that simple strategy to accumulate my seven figure fortune.

So why reveal my methods now? Well, I'm semi retired and I've made enough money so that my kids do not need to work one more day in their lives (if they so desire). I've had my blessings and now I want to help others succeed as well, this is my way to give back.

Now look, 99% of the folks who try to make it on the Internet follow the same rout, the same set of activities. They all move in one big herd. Listen, In the highly competitive online arena, when you do the same things as anyone else you don't stand a chance to succeed - you are doomed.

In order to win the internet battles you must go off the beaten path, you need to do something different, you need a competitive edge - and that is where my simple strategy comes into play. It gives you that "unfair advantage" to boost your sales, pile up profits and leave your competitors in the dust.

When a soldier goes into battle he seeks to equip himself with the best weapons he could lay his hands on. The same goes for the internet battles. The single most important factor in utilizing my strategy successfully is equipping yourself with the right tools and services. The magic word is 'Automation'. You need to have the best tools and you need to know how to put them to best use. This is critical, some of the tools that I'll show you can actually heart you if not used correctly.

Look, in order to make money on the internet you need to get noticed by the search engines and you need to climb up the search engines result pages (SERPs). Unfortunately Google and the other search engines give preference to large and established sites. The little guy with a relatively new or small website does not stand a chance. You could of course go the "natural" rout. That will take you about 5 years to establish a site that will be liked by Google. I don't know about you, but I prefer to start making money with a new site much earlier than that. That is why you need to use some special tools, to take some unconventional measures - you need to be a little more creative.

As a matter of fact, one of the best kept secrets of the cyber-millionaires is what tools they use and, more importantly, how they make use of them for maximum benefit.

Here's a list of the tools and services that I use while executing my strategy, later on I'll show you exactly how the strategy works and how these tools integrates perfectly within it to come up with the easiest, fastest, most effective way of making money online:

1. Keyword Research Tool: Keyword Canine - a multi-featured tool for niche discovery, keyword research and backlink analysis (for more details see here: http://www.liraz.com/canine)

2. Hosting Service: HostGator - a reliable web hosting. Has some extra features that makes it suitable for internet marketing activities. (for more details see here: http://www.liraz.com/hostgator)

3. Wordpress Theme: Thesis - much more than a theme, it's more of a design and template manager for Wordpress. Most suitable for a business site that is meant to be ranked high on the search engines. (for more details see here: http://www.liraz.com/thesis)

4. Content Creator: Article Builder - **produces high quality unique articles built around the topics and**

keywords that you give it. (for more details see here: http://www.liraz.com/articlebuilder)

5. Email Marketing Tool: Weber - automatically manage all email marketing activities: creates sign-up forms, collects and manages subscribers, sends out scheduled emails and more. Powerful yet very easy to use. (for more details see here: http://www.liraz.com/aweber)

6. Article Spinner: The Best spinner - a multi-featured tool for creating multiple versions of an article that will be seen as unique in the search engines. (for more details see here: http://www.liraz.com/bestspiner)

7. Links Building knowledge: Link Building Course - a comprehensive link building learning framework that is constantly updated to reflect the most recent effective link building strategies (for more details see here: http://www.liraz.com/linkbuilding)

8. Manual Link Building: Rank Crew - an affordable and reliable manual link building service (for more details see here: http://www.liraz.com/rankcrew).

9. Automatic Directory Submission: DeepLinkerPro - automate the creation of manual directory links, allows the use of varied anchor text and also to drip feed the submissions over time to make it all look as natural as possible (for more details see here: http://www.liraz.com/deeplinker)

10. Automatic Link Builder: Senuke - a powerful

backlinking tool which has been designed to assist with the time consuming task of creating a large number of links (for more details see here: http://www.liraz.com/senuke)

11. Backlinks Indexer and Booster: Backlink Booster - automatically increases the power of the backlinks to a website. It's both a backlink indexer aiming to get the backlinks indexed faster, and also a backlink booster to help boost the amount of link juice each of the backlinks sends to a website (for more details see here: http://www.liraz.com/backlinkbooster)

Now, in order to take full advantage of my strategy you need to be familiar with basic Internet business concepts. The next chapter features a list of tips and ideas that touches on various internet business topics. This is basic stuff - if you are new to internet business these tips can help with your first steps in the field and also serve as an introduction. If you have some Internet business background you may want to skip the next chapter and hop right to chapter 3 where I start revealing the formula that made me an internet millionaire.

2. Internet Business Beginners Tips and Ideas

The following list of tips is meant to provide new comers with basic Internet business advice to help improve their initial online business activities. It can also serve as an introduction to online business. Note that these tips are not necessary related to my formula but rather constitute general internet business advice. If you are an experienced online marketer you may want to skip this chapter and go directly to the next one where I start explaining my simple, yet highly effective, formula of making lots of money online.

Now here are the tips:

1. Survey site visitors about what they'd like to see on the website. This builds a relationship with your site visitors; they think you care about what they want, and are trying to give them what they ask for. A survey can also give you feedback about a product or a service.

2. A website's HTML tag is one of its most important features. It tells the world who you are. Tags affect your search engine rankings, and the title tag will be visible to potential visitors. Having mismatched titles and information is one of the quickest ways to drive people away from your site.

3. To have an internet marketing site that is truly worthwhile, it is important that you are always combating attrition. If you have a potential customer, you must hook them in whatever way possible. If your website is not clean,

they may turn away. If your site is not interesting, they may turn away.

4. When marketing your site, try to avoid looking at the ranking of your pages for at least the first few months. Checking on your progress may cause you to become discouraged. Results do not happen immediately, and seeing slow progress might cause you to throw in the towel. Just keep your head down, work hard, and then check in.

5. Using a double opt-in method for your email marketing lists ensures that you are reaching those customers who are truly interested in your product. While a double opt-in procedure seems like a barrier to creating a marketing list, it does mean that everyone on your list was willing to follow at least one link back to your site.

6. Pay attention to the design of your website. Use attractive colors and a menu that is easy to navigate. Visitors will spend more time on a website with nice colors and an original design. They are also more likely to remember your website and come back to it later. Make sure your menu is clear so that people can find what they want without getting frustrated.

7. Create a blog and offer an RSS feed. Blogging is an effective way to market your business and you can quickly and easily add new content without having to learn any HTML. An RSS feeds allows you to syndicate your content to other websites so that you can increase your business's exposure.

8. Be your website's harshest critic. Much the same as every mother views her child as the best in the world, a website owner is similarly biased towards their site. No website is perfect, and the first step to improvement is admitting this fact. From there you can pinpoint areas where you can make things better.

9. An important tip regarding Internet marketing is to use press releases as a way to spread news about your company and also draw traffic to your site. This is a great way to advertise because not only does it promote your product but it also will improve your legitimacy and search engine ranking.

10. A great way to bring prestige to your site is to get high-quality information and respected interviews with people who have a relation to what your site is selling. You either provide the interviews in audio or video format. The interview will show your visitors that you are connected with the experts in your niche and increase your reputation as a trusted authority.

11. When designing your website, do not omit important details no matter how trivial they may seem at first. Every page should include the site name, slogan or logo, and a very basic description of your product or service offering. This ensures that visitors know exactly who you are and what you sell. This is especially useful if a visitor was somehow directed to your site by another website or link.

12. An important tip regarding Internet marketing is to be

sure that you make a strong effort to advertise the speed that the order will be processed and shipped. This is important because many people have now gotten accustomed to extremely quick processing and delivery. Even if you cannot compete with larger companies, it is important to be as quick and efficient as possible.

13. The first goal of every good internet marketing plan, is to convert website viewers into paying customers. Once a visitor has made this jump and bought something from you, a brief thank-you communication (most commonly an email) is a good way to demonstrate your appreciation. This should be a message completely free of up-sell advertising, and also separate from order confirmation messages.

14. Try rewarding repeat customers or customers who spend over a certain dollar amount with something like a temporary or permanent discount towards their future purchases. You could even have it set for certain times to encourage them to come back soon and purchase more to take advantage of that discount.

15. A lot of people are afraid to get into marketing on the web because of the failure factor. Knowing that you may not succeed is a huge deterrent for many people. Just know that the success stories out there are anything but rare, and if you follow wise advice like the tips provided in this book, you can become one of those happy endings.

16. In the world of internet marketing you will always be presented with the opportunity to take advantage of a

popular scam. It is important that you resist this with everything possible. Maintaining a profitable company overtime requires a company that has the trust and respect of its customers. This cannot be reached through shady or sneaky methods.

17. Be as detailed as possible when marketing a product. Studies show that large percentages of the population need profuse explanations about the benefits of the products they are thinking of buying in order to be persuaded. If customers genuinely believe the marketing, they will be much more willing to buy the product. Researchers have found that many people will trust a website with several paragraphs of information about a product over a website that is very succinct.

18. Pay attention to the different types of voices discussing your brand (such as consumers, potential consumers and industry pundits) and, with discretion, respond to any misconceptions or problems they may have. This will help you look like you care about the thoughts of everyday people or generally an understanding of your brand's strategies in the industry, helping your brand seem more personable.

19. Keep in mind that the internet is always evolving and that new websites and new ways of communicating are always appearing. You should try new techniques for every new tool that appears. Some new tools are definitely not good for marketing, but you have to try until you find something that works.

INTERNET BUSINESS SUCCESS FORMULA

20. Hold contests for users to submit content that you will incorporate into your online marketing efforts somehow. Users will not only feel like you respect their opinions but they will see that they have the opportunity to personally take a role in improving your brand, essentially doing the work of figuring out what consumers want for you.

21. When you get a customer on your site, it is important that you turn them into a lead. If your site does not accomplish this, then you will never be able to make the profit that you wish for. It is vitally important that your site attracts people and then persuades them to purchase your product.

22. It is important to make the internet marketing experience for your customer as pleasant as possible by providing a website that doesn't look cheap. If you can't afford a professional website design, consider taking a low cost course at a local county college and spruce up your site with the tips that you learn.

23. One way to promote your internet business is by publishing an e-zine on topics relating to your business, and inviting people to subscribe to it. As your readership grows, your reputation as a trusted source in your field will improve as well. When you gain your readers' trust, your readers will be more willing to seek your services when they need an expert.

24. Focus on the level of content that you include on each page. It is much better if you have an average quantity of

great content than filler, which simply repeats your keyword over and over and says nothing more. Put emphasis on the content and quality of your webpage for ultimate results.

25. Once you have your domain and host in place and are ready to go the next step in your future internet marketing success, Implement your plan for the design of your website. You should consider your market and fashion the actual website accordingly. There are many tools available to assist you in designing your site.

26. Concentrate your efforts on the pages that really matter. Every website has a few pages dedicated to disclaimers, policies or a contact form. If people want to see these pages, they will look for them. Create links to the pages that you want people to see: your home page or a page that presents your products.

27. Participate in online discussion forums related to your niche and include a link to your website in your forum signature. This activity can get you lots of quality backlinks to your website which can increase your search engine rank. You may also get a lot of relevant visitors to your website from the forums.

28. Before implementing your idea, brainstorm. Brainstorming will allow your whole marketing team to inject certain thoughts towards your site and can serve as a valuable tool and an insightful start to your project. Do not discount any one's opinion, because it could lead to a lot of

profit in the future for your business.

29. A well-optimized website is one with flawless CSS language. This is due to search engines becoming more and more discriminating in their indexing procedures. Today search engines examine the style sheets along with all the rest of a website's content and machinery. Up-to-date website owners will use free tools to check the validity of their CSS pages. A broken CSS page can cost a website valuable search engine ranking.

30. An important tip regarding Internet marketing is to be sure that prices for goods that you offer not only are competitive, but also do not undercut the entire market. This is important, because you are partially responsible for the value of the product you sell. If you offer it at a lower cost, then others will follow, and you lessen the overall value.

31. You should be willing to go the extra mile to satisfy your online business's customers. This is important to a sensible internet marketing strategy. While online customers' demands may seem unreasonable to you at first, remember that every customer online is a model. If you make them happy, more customers in the same situation will soon follow.

32. You should look for new products that are not available in stores yet. People will not be able to compare prices with other offers and they will also be interested by the novelty of the product. Make sure you explain why the product is

necessary, and why it will become very popular soon. Try the product yourself first to see if there is really a future for it.

33. If you would like to attract new customers without spending a lot of money, you should research referral marketing. Most referral marketing systems offer their services for a low cost and the amount of money they can make your website is significant. Because the internet makes tracking customer behavior easy, you can market products to customers in a hyper-specified and effective way.

34. Know your weaknesses. Delegating work that you tend to put off, or may not do so well, is often a very good idea. If you haven't updated your web site with new material in a while because you just don't enjoy the task, perhaps you should consider having someone else write content for you.

35. As important as the content on your website is, the appearance may play an even bigger role in your success. If you do not take the time to design a website format that is inviting and pleasing to the eye, many visitors may just back right out of your site and move on to a different site.

36. Sometimes, it is very difficult for a new customer to understand some of the terms on your site. Therefore, it is important for you to include a glossary of a terms page, dedicated to explaining the difficult words or phrases. This will aid in improving your customer's overall experience on your website.

37. Learn what target marketing is, and how you can use it. Research the best methods available using blogs, books, or even target marketing companies. Use these to figure out who your target market really is, what you want from them, and how you can attain it. Target marketing is very reliable.

38. If you are trying to sell something online it is important to be detailed. Your customers are at a disadvantage because they cannot see, feel, touch, and/or try your product, they are relying upon good details in order to make an educated decision as to whether they wish to purchase it or not.

39. When trying to sell a product online, it is important to make it easy for your customer to buy your product. Regardless of whether your site is just simple text with a few pictures or a large professionally designed online store, your customer needs to know how and where to make a purchase. If that information is too difficult to find, you will lose a majority of your sales.

40. Getting feedback on your advertisements is a great way to cater specifically to the market of your choice. Make sure that you're always attempting to seek outside opinions on your marketing campaign. Never be shy and always ask customers what they think about your business and what you can do to improve it.

41. One Internet marketing tactic that can pay off is partnering with complementary businesses. This means steering traffic from the website to suppliers of a product

or service that complements the websites business without competing with it. The partner supplier returns the favor. In this way non-competitive businesses can tap into one pool of potential customers that share interest in their products.

42. Utilizing social networks is a great way to enhance your internet marketing campaigns. You can find various tools online to help you post to all major search engines, which will help you save time. Not only will this be a lot less work, but it also ensures that you will reach a much larger audience.

43. Consider giving discount coupons or exclusive special offers to customers after their first purchase through your website. This is an excellent internet marketing tactic for encouraging repeat business. It offers customers something of undeniable value - but only if they return to buy from you again. You can make more money and make your customers happy!

44. Your internet marketing messages should create incentives for customers to place their order as soon as possible. This is a common and effective strategy that creates a temporary window of opportunity that most consumers view as a blink-and-you'll-miss-it affair. The incentive could be free shipping, free gift wrapping, or a free product for the first 500 people who place an order.

45. Make it very easy for people to subscribe to your site by entering their email addresses. This may not seem as

popular as it was a few years back, but there are many people that still check their email daily and they like to see newsletters and information there, regularly.

46. An important tip regarding Internet marketing is to be sure that you test your site among the most popular Internet browsers in order to assure compatibility. The very least you should do if you find an issue that cannot be fixed is to write a script stating what issues can occur in specific browsers and what browsers your recommend.

47. Don't forget the call to action. Every single piece of communication from you should include a link to your website, as well as a suggestion to "learn more", "get a free sample" and other enticing statements that make your visitors want to click over to your site. This will urge them to go further and result in higher viewers and higher sales.

48. To make more sales, you should target your customers carefully. Advertise products related to your website. Think about what kind of people would visit your website, and what kind of products they might be interested in. Choose products that you can actually sell and target your audience carefully when advertising.

49. Provide a webinar that not only focuses on a problem or difficult scenario within your niche, but also comes close to solving the problem. You then enhance the solution with a product (your product or an affiliate product) that will complete the solution and be the ultimate answer to the problem.

50. Track information other than your website numbers. Keeping a strong log of how many people email, call, or snail-mail you can be beneficial to showing you how many visitors you actually have. Having knowledge of these statistics can give you the information you need to increase your visitors and buyers.

51. If your e-newsletters aren't driving the traffic you want, take the time to learn how to develop an engaging e-newsletter. Look at the successful e-newsletters that competing brands are offering and cherry pick some of the better ideas that you see in them. You can then develop those ideas into your own voice.

52. Send out an email or place a coupon on your website allowing your customers to give out a discount code to introduce their friends and co-workers to your products. Allow existing customers to use one for themselves, too, so you reward their loyalty and show that you value their continuing business.

53. When building up an email list for your Internet marketing efforts, you really need to try to avoid preformed mailing lists. And if you do get a mailing list that you didn't put together yourself through volunteer addresses, you at least need to make sure that you're targeting a very, very specific market. Once you're seen as a spammer, it's all over.

54. Tracking your customers is a great way to see when they're coming, when they're going, and how they're getting

to your site. Find resources to help you uncover this data and practice reading the data so that you can quickly and efficiently spot trends and follow them to improve your business.

55. See if you can get your site linked from a .edu or .gov site. The search engines rank content and links coming from these domains with a lot of weight and credibility. Having your link included in one of those sites will get you credibility by association. These links can be difficult to get but are worth a try.

56. Use catchy slogans and attractive logos on your website so that your customers remember you. Short slogans and logos tend to stick in people's minds, and can be the way they remember you. If you can make your logo and slogan memorable, people are more likely to come back. Slogans can cause people to your website to others too.

57. If your customer's sign up for a newsletter or email service, make sure that you do not spam them. Spamming can be really frustrating, which can lead to angry customers. When someone is interested in your product, they will leverage off of the knowledge they acquire, as spamming typically does not work.

58. Keep the size of the pictures on your site small to reduce the time that it takes to load on a customer's computer. They will have the ability to increase the size of an object if it is too small. Your goal should be to reel the customer into your site by any means necessary.

59. Intrigue your visitors by offering a section of your site that requires an account and password to get into. There is something about secret areas that really intrigues customers into wanting to find out what they are missing. It can be regarded as trying to access a hidden treasure on your site.

60. Create links to other sites that have given you positive reviews. This will increase your credibility with the public. You can link to the sites that sing your praises both in your ad and also elsewhere on your site. Tell the public to check out what others who have linked to you have to say.

61. Let your customers set the price for your products when they are products that you've been holding onto for some time because they are not selling. Don't be afraid to entertain reasonable offers via your email or web form. You might even want to accept offers of barter for their products or services.

62. Make sure it's easy for customers to unsubscribe from your emails. While it may lose you a few readers, if it's easy to unsubscribe you may not lose them as customers. If it's a hassle, customers will get annoyed and stop using your website all together. Not only that, but they may mark the emails as "spam" getting your emails caught up in spam filters across the provider.

63. Always project a positive attitude. Even if you are marketing a solution to a problem, focus on the advantages of your solution rather than the pain or inconvenience of the problem. People viewing your website already know all

about their difficulties and they would like to know how you can make everything better for them.

64. Wherever a webmaster solicits comments from his or her visitors - on blogs, in forums, through product reviews - responding to those comments can greatly increase visitor interest. Visitors who receive attention are more likely to trust the webmaster. From an internet marketing point of view, visitors who trust, are more likely to become customers who buy.

65. Choose targeted marketing campaigns instead of massive advertising blitzes. By personalizing your message and targeting it to your likely buyers, you can send the message that your product is useful and necessary and that you care about your consumers. If you go for a massive blitz, you will dehumanize your customers and make them resent you for "spamming".

66. An important tip regarding Internet marketing is to be sure that you judge the content and layout of your own site as though it belonged to someone else. If you have issues being subjective then it may be best to let someone else either layout decisions or at least confide in them first.

67. In order to appeal to a larger audience you should have copies of your web site available in different languages. If someone cannot read English then it is highly unlikely they will want to buy anything from you, so you have to cater to them in order to get their business.

68. You want your customers to feel that you can be

trusted and you have nothing to hide so it is a good idea to allow them to have your actual business address. Sometimes people feel as if those who only have P.O. Box addresses available are hiding something from them.

69. An important tip regarding Internet marketing is to come across as human as possible. This is important because people are much more willing to trust a company if they can relate to them and see real humans that they are interacting with. Put a video of yourself or a tour of your work space on your site.

70. Get involved with the Chamber of Commerce in your area, since many of them have an opt-in list. Email all of the members that are on the list and invite them to view your website and sign up for your newsletter. Offer incentives, if you want to get more of them to take the bait.

71. Go to Google blog search and look for your company or brand name. Subscribe to that search result using Google Reader. This will let you see what people are saying about your company, and get a general feeling about their attitude towards your business. Use the negative comments to change some areas that customers are having issues with.

72. Try offering your customers an affiliate program option when they purchase from you. This can help you because if they sign up for your affiliate program then they have one of your ads on their site. This can lead to tons more traffic and many more sales on your site.

73. There's one magic word in internet marketing: "fast".

Potential customers these days are looking for a fast solution to their problems, and if you can find a way to incorporate the word "fast" into your sales copy and website they will be more likely to buy. Let them know that you can solve their problem and you can do it quickly.

74. A great way to get you recognized is to cater to a market within a market. We all know about niche markets but there are actually smaller markets inside of every niche. Instead of catering to an encompassing market or even a mid-sized market, target your approach to a concentrated market with high traffic rates. There is less competition here and your site will live on the front page.

75. Make a commercial! While some people don't like the idea of making commercials, studies show that they are much more effective at influencing customer buying habits than the printed word. There are low-budget options to use, just make sure the commercial is entirely relevant. With a little effort and investment, you can increase your consumer base with just a few words.

76. A great internet marketing tip is to do a little bit of research on keywords. It's important to know which keywords are popular because they have enormous potential to drive traffic to your web site. A good idea is to generate pages of content on your site for different keywords.

77. To attract more visitors to your site, make "top 10" and "best of" lists. People love reading lists, and providing

content people want to read will allow you to market products more efficiently. Take the time to go through your affiliate's products and make a list of some of the best they have to offer. It will pay off in the long run!

78. When you are writing a blog it is best to write about things that you already know about. Trying to sound like you have expertise in a field that you do not know will only serve to make you look bad to all the people that are reading what you have to say.

79. Err on the side of caution if you are unsure of what font or style to choose for your website. Not everyone will have perfect sight, especially the older visitors to your page, so use a font that is clear, large and legible if you want to improve the overall experience of your visitors.

80. If you've made the decision to market your business online, avoid making the common mistake of using a free website. These websites include ads, banners and frames that clutter your website and have nothing to do with your product. Some of these are pop-ups that may be difficult to close and can block access to certain parts of your webpage. You are also stuck with a domain name that is hard to remember and does not look professional. If your business begins to grow, the space you're allotted may not be enough. In addition, when the server for one of these sites goes down, it may take days for the problem to be resolved.

81. Promote your business, large or small, by harnessing

the power of social networks. Even if you do not sell products directly through these sites, customers are sure to appreciate the ease of providing feedback through messages. You also can use the networks to announce product releases or news related to your business in a way that seems more personal than press releases.

82. Make a website for your business and keep it up-to-date. If a customer or potential client is interested in your business, the first thing they'll often look at is your website. You want to include any relevant information about your business on that site, make it look nice, and above all, make sure it's user friendly!

83. Fresh, lively and informative content, is key to any successful website, so take a look at your website's content on a regular basis. Don't let it grow stale and out of date. Add new content on a regular basis, so that you'll attract more visitors who want to see what's new.

84. For better results, promote products that are unique. If you are promoting the same thing as a thousand other sites, you'll find less results coming from those items. Your customer may be interested in your product, but they've probably already gone to it from a different site. Find items that are unique and less heavily promoted by other sites. Set yourself apart and see bigger results.

85. Brand yourself up. Make a logo, a saying, or even a simple title that will carry into everything you do. When people start to recognize your brand, success is on the way.

Market your website just like you would a product: acknowledge the shortfalls, but be sure to praise the uniqueness.

86. Become the expert in your field, in order to increase your internet business success. Use webinars or podcasts to educate current and potential customers. Write informational articles for distribution online. When you become the person people turn to for answers, that will drive more traffic and business to your site.

87. A 302 redirect should only be used to mask unwieldy long URLs. A 302 tells the engine that this redirect is only a temporary change, and the original should not be removed from their indexes. They are useful for making your URL more user friendly, but be wary as they are frequently used by spammers.

88. It is always wise to include keywords in all HTML title tags. By doing this, search engines will be more apt to factor them into search result calculations, thus facilitating higher page rankings for your content. In keeping with this theory, it is also important to include effective keywords in tags, titles and descriptors relating to videos you place online.

89. Try your best to make sure that your advertising stands out. If your ads look humdrum and discernible from others then people will assume your product is not unique. Capitalizing particular words like "free" and "now" or putting them in bold font is sure to catch the customer's

eye.

90. An important tip regarding Internet marketing is to obtain an online social networking and microblogging account. This is a great way to get news or information out to subscribers, and also a great way to link back to your site. It is important to remain as credible and professional as possible through any media that you use.

91. Be very specific when choosing the products you want to market to your audience. General items like napkins, printer paper, or socks may be used by everyone who visits your website, but that's not what they're coming to you to find. Target the products to the specific topic of your website. For example, if you're a tech review blog, link to the latest, greatest electronics.

92. If anyone famous or well-known is a customer of yours or have used a product of yours, make certain to publish a list of their names for all of your customers to see. This gives you some serious credibility and makes customers want to trust you more when purchasing from your site.

93. A fast customer service department can have a huge positive impact on an internet marketing strategy. Online business moves quickly and online customers are quick to grow dissatisfied. By addressing their concerns as rapidly as possible, successful business websites maintain a positive online reputation that can preserve and even expand their customer base.

94. Put something unique in your site. This can be a very

effective means of increasing traffic to your pages. The visitors then usually end up checking out other parts of your sites which eventually sends it up the search engine rankings.

95. Don't clutter up your content with advertisements. A reader visits your website with intent on gaining the content you have posted, not being bombarded with multiple ads. Make sure you have just enough to get your point across. Having too many will actually drive readers away from your site, which is counter-intuitive.

96. One of the most appealing aspects of your personality that you can instill in your site is humor. Make sure that you keep things business professional, but including a joke here and there will never hurt. Inserting humor into your communication with customers makes for a very light and fun level of dialogue.

97. Use social bookmarking sites to your advantage. Unlike regular bookmarking, which saves to the browser, social bookmarking saves to their personal page. Many have an option to bookmark a page publicly, allowing their peers to see who they have bookmarked. This is a great way to increase your visibility among your target audience.

98. Try to get your business listed in directories that cater to people in a certain target market. If you have a real estate business, you would not want to be in a directory filled with lawyers. Find directories that are specific to whatever type of business you specialize in.

99. Add high ticket items to your list of items you sell. It takes the same amount of effort to sell a high priced product as it does to sell a low priced one. You may be pleasantly surprised at the people that will invest in a product that is higher priced.

100. Make sure you do set up a twitter account to increase your internet marketing and presence. The platform is different than Facebook so make sure you spend some time learning how it works. It can be a great tool to share your business and interact with your customer base.

101. Visit the sites of your competitors. This will allow you to see what you're up against, but it can also give you ideas about what you can do a little better or a little differently. You can use their websites for ideas about content for your own site and blog.

3. Locating Profit-Driving Keywords

The way my formula works is simple. You focus on creating quick little sites that each target a laser targeted long-tail keywords. Once you complete one site you quickly move onto the next. So you don't want to spend too much time on any one site. This way you create, one by one, an army of passive income websites that keep producing cash for years.

I'll show you exactly how to create and promote your first money making website, than you just rinse and repeat to create as many websites as you wish, the more sites you create the more money you make. The only limit is how far you want to go.

Now let's not waste any more time and move directly to the first component of the strategy which deals with deciding on the keywords your site is going to target. This is a crucial decision and a fundamental part of achieving success online. You could do everything else perfectly, but target the wrong keywords and your site will be a total failure. in this chapter I'll tell you exactly what to look for when searching for good solid keywords.

Most Internet Marketing "experts" and the self-proclaimed gurus will tell you to use the Google Keyword Tool (now called: "Keyword Planner" and is only available to Adwords account users) for your keyword research. This is a big mistake! if you only use the Google tool you'll end up going in circles with the rest of the herd achieving no success.

Why? although the Google tool will provide you with a nice list of several hundred keyword variations, it will tell you nothing as to the competitiveness of the terms. You have no clue as to how hard it will be to rank in the search engines for any specific term. This is critical. Most newbies will choose a term from the Google Tool that is too competitive and end up hitting a brick wall. You certainly don't want to be spending any time or money building a site that will never rank in the SE's.

In order to implement the strategy successfully you need to utilize for your keyword research a tool named Keyword Canine (If the link doesn't work, copy and paste the following URL into a browser: **www.liraz.com/canine**).

Keyword Canine (KC) will also provide you with a nice list of several hundred keyword variations but it goes beyond the Google Tool in that it will also analyze the competitiveness of each keyword variation. This is crucial and that is where you gain your "unfair advantage" over the 99% that only use the Google Tool.

How does KC do it? it has a special algorithm in its backend that looks at the top 10 Google search results for your chosen keyword and produces an accurate analysis in the form of "Very Easy, Easy, Moderate, Hard or Fierce" so you can literally plug in your keyword and get an instant answer.

Keyword Canine has a ton of additional features that can help you as an Internet marketer but for the purpose the implementation of my strategy, the competition analysis is what we need.

I'm not going to walk you here thru the steps of conducting a keyword research with Keyword Canine as they have pretty good tutorials explaining everything. Simply sign for the service and follow their instructions.

Now let's see what properties a keyword must have in order to make us the most money.

For starter it has to be of a commercial value. This relates to our business model, the way we monetize our site. I will elaborate on this in a later chapter but for now I can tell you that our income will come from two sources:

a. Google AdSense ads.

b. Affiliate Programs

To maximize our income from those two we need to look for keywords in markets that has AdSense advertisers and affiliate programs that are willing to pay us top dollars. in the appendix you can find a list of the 50 best paying affiliate marketing niches. These are the markets that has a high concentration of AdSense advertisers and affiliate programs that are willing to pay top Dollars for your referrals. If you plan to tap any of these niches you must take into consideration that these are also the most competitive ones. However, I think it is still possible to find gem keywords in these areas provided you do your keyword research right. Alternatively you can look at other, less competitive, niches and still make good money as long as you take into consideration their commercial value.

Another property that you want to consider when looking for good keywords is the search volume. Obviously, even a #1 ranking isn't going to do you any good at all if nobody searches for the keyword that you rank for. I would say that the minimum search volume you should look for is 500 monthly searches (Keyword Canine shows you the search volume right next to the keywords in the list). Some will say that this is too low to target, however I had many successes with pages targeting close to this number of monthly searches.

The next property you need to consider for a good keyword is how competitive it is, how hard it will be to have it ranked in the first page of Google's search results. This is critical, however if you use Keyword Canine it will do the competition analysis for you and come with a recommendation in the form of "Very Easy, Easy, Moderate, Hard or Fierce". I would not go beyond "easy" with a new site.

So to summarize, in order to find a good keyword you need to consider:

* Commercial value

* Search volume

* competition strength

How many keywords should you target in one site? Some

will tell you that you need to look for several terms and optimize each page in the site for a different term. This is not how my strategy works. For the small niche sites that we create it is best to dedicate each site to only one keyword and direct all our Search Engine Optimization (SEO) efforts towards the main page that is optimized for that keyword. We don't want to dilute our efforts by targeting several keywords in a site. With this concept in mind we don't want to waste our time looking for other keywords that will not rank anyway. Your time is better spent working on your linking structure (discussed later) or researching new keywords for new sites.

4. Creating a Stream of income

The success formula business model is based on 2 sources of income:

a. Google AdSense ads.

b. Affiliate Programs

Which is better? there is no clear answer to this question. Some niches will produce better with affiliate programs while others with AdSense, you should test on a niche by niche bases. Usually you'll make more money with an affiliate site, unfortunately there may be many instances where you will find a good niche with keywords that can be easily ranked but no suitable affiliate program, in this case you'll use AdSense ads, and by the way, this will happen to you a lot.

Once you find a good keyword to target you start looking for an affiliate program that will go with this site. As a rule of thumb you should always prefer to promote digital products (eBooks, software, online services, etc.) over physical products. Why? because digital products come with higher margins which in most cases translate into higher commissions to the site owner.

Where can you find good affiliate programs to promote?

Your first bet should be the Clickbank Marketplace (https://accounts.clickbank.com/marketplace.htm)

Clickbank offers thousands of products, look for products

that are 100% relevant to your niche and has a credible sales page.

If you can't find a suitable product at Clickbank try one of the following affiliate program directories:

Commission Junction **(http://www.cj.com)**

Affiliatetips.com (http://www.affiliatetips.com)

AssociatePrograms.com (http://www.associateprograms.com/directory/)

Affiliatesdirectory.com (http://affiliatesdirectory.com/directory)

If you still can't find a suitable affiliate program try a Google search that combines your keyword with the word "affiliates" and other similar variations. Sometimes this works and you will find one or more good affiliate offers for your niche.

If all of the above does not work and you can't find an affiliate program that is relevant to your target niche, monetize your site with AdSense ads. This is not necessarily a bad thing. I had AdSense ads that produced $5, $6 and even $9 per click.

Anyway, don't ever be tempted to post affiliate links that are not fully relevant to your target keywords! this will never produce satisfactory results.

Where should you place your affiliate links and AdSense

ads on the page? The best spot would be right below the top article title and above the article body, if you are using Wordpress it would be directly below the post title and above the post content. This would be the spot that will by far produce the best results.

As for the AdSense ads, I always match the background and border of the ad with the background of the theme where the ad will be placed and I recommend you do the same - my tests show that this increases the effectiveness of the ads. You can use a plug-in for Firefox and Chrome called [Colorzilla](http://www.colorzilla.com/) (http://www.colorzilla.com/) to help you do this quickly.

Another good option for the affiliate links is to embed them within the text, preferably towards the top part of the article.

As for affiliate links, my tests show that reviews and text ads will, in most cases, outperform banners. I guess some folks simply ignore banners altogether. I seldom use banners to promote affiliate offers, I've always found effective ways to present affiliate offers with text only. I will be the first to admit that my pages are not very pretty, but hey, I'm not in the business of creating cute pages, I am in the business of making money, and for this my "not pretty" pages are doing very well.

Below is an example of affiliate links embedded within an article:

> ### Free Car Insurance Deals
>
> #### Here's How to Get Free Car Insurance Deals
>
> So you are interested in locating free car insurance deals. Well, I will show you now not just how to find those free deals but rather how to find the cheapest car insurance rate that is available in your area.
>
> The single most critical factor in getting the best auto insurance deals is shopping around for as many quotes as you can. How many? you should go for at least 5 quotes from different auto insurance companies, less than that will simply not do the job.
>
> Now, the problem is that shopping around for five quotes can be a tedious and time consuming task - well, not anymore, now it can be much easier for you.
>
> We've reviewed numerous quoting services to bring you the best two. Each of the following free services can provide you with several competing quotes from various companies, thus enabling you to compare and pinpoint on the best rate that is available for your location. in order to maximize your chances of getting the best rate possible we recommend you use both services:
>
> InsurMe - May save you hundreds on your car insurance. Simply enter in your zip code and get free quotes from providers in your local area that offer great rates.
>
> Kanetix - Provides multiple company insurance rates, see how companies compete for your business. Offers great rates from quality insurers.
>
> Once you have in your hands several quotes, you can use The Car Insurance Price

Here's is an example of affiliate links in a review format placed under the title of an article. By the way, I've used this format, "The 5 Best ...", multiple times with various niches. Over the years this format proved to be very profitable for me.

> **Car Insurance Information Center**
>
> **7 Day Car Insurance, Compare to Get Low Cost Rate**
>
> **The 5 Best Car Insurance Quotes Providers**
> We've reviewed dozens of auto insurance companies, brokers and agents to bring you this elite list of brands with the best free quotes online and very cheap rates. We recommend you get a quote from each company so that you will be able to compare and get the best rate. This comparison will allow you to save as much as $500 and more on your vehicle insurance.
>
> 1. Car Insurance Finders - May save you hundreds on your car insurance. Simply enter in your zip code and get free quotes from providers in your local area that offer the best rates.
> 2. USInsurance - Simply fill out the quick form and this system will match you up with the cheapest offers in real-time. You get low cost custom tailored quotes within minutes.
> 3. InsureMe - Provides multiple company insurance rates, see how companies compete for your business. Offers great rates from quality insurers.
> 4. 2Insure4Less - Provides comparison quotes which can be purchased immediately, offers great rates.
> 5. Kanetix - Offers one of the easiest to use, and most 'consumer-friendly' instant insurance comparison service available.
>
> For many people, it is not easy to get a large amount to cover something such as insurance coverage. It could be a significant wide range of dollars to cover at one time, therefore, the choice of no deposit car insurance is often rather appealing.
>
> No deposit car insurance implies that you get instant auto insurance protection straight away, when the insurance policy is put over your car, so you do not need to pay anything in advance. You are able to pay the insurance policy on a monthly base in payments; nevertheless, you may have to offer a credit card for guarantee that you submit several

Build an Email List

The biggest sin committed by internet marketers is not building an email list made of emails collected from visitors and customers. In order to maximize the profit potential of your site you need to create an email list. Fortunately, all the aspects of building and maintaining a list can be, and should be, automated. Selling to your list is the easiest money you're going to make.

Now I'm not going to teach you basic Email marketing here, you'll find plenty of resources online. However, here are 4 important points that you should consider:

1. Build an opt-in form and integrate it into your home

page. Place it "above the fold," so visitors can see it immediately and don't have to scroll down.

2. Offer a lead magnet, something that has value that you offer in exchange for the visitor's email address. This could be a free eBook, a special report, a webinar, a list of tips, Etc. You have to tailor the offer to fit your niche so that you keep your list targeted, this is important.

3. Use [Weber](www.liraz.com/aweber) (If the link doesn't work, copy and paste the following URL into a browser: **www.liraz.com/aweber**) to manage your list building and marketing activities. Aweber is the industry standard. It's extremely powerful yet very easy to use, most of the successful internet marketers use it. Working with Aweber is a breath, it will automate all your email marketing activities: creating your sign-up forms, collecting and managing subscribers, sending out scheduled emails and more.

4. Email marketing is about creating a relation with your visitors and customers, it's about trust. Do not abuse it by spamming your list with frequent blatant sales offers. Send them at list 3 useful, content filled, emails for each email that contains a sales offer.

5. Creating a Money Making Website

Once you have chosen your keywords you are ready to build your site. For your domain name you should strive for an exact match domain (EMD) if available. So if your keyword is 'women car insurance' you'll go for www.womencarinsurance.com. if this is not available try the .net, .info or any other TLD that happens to be available.

EMD domains used to get you a big advantage with Google - but not anymore. Unfortunately Google has changed their algo regarding EMDs but it can still get you some extra points, and of course anything that Google gives we are willing to take.

As for the hosting service I highly recommend you use HostGator (If the link doesn't work, copy and paste the following URL into a browser: **www.liraz.com/hostgator**), They are reliable, responsible and very suitable for internet marketing activities.

The cheapest and fastest way to build an effective niche site is to use Wordpress. and by the way, HostGator is probably the easiest web hosting platform to install Wordpress on. Using a few clicks of the mouse, your HostGator-hosted Wordpress site will be up and ready in less than five minutes. look for instructions at their site.

Once Wordpress is installed on your server there are some modifications that you need to make to the site.

First you need to set Wordpress to present SEO Friendly Permalinks. Although we don't' concentrate on the internal pages of our site, they often can rank in the SE's. So it is very important to set a good URL structure. Once logged into Wordpress, Click "Settings" then "Permalinks" and change it from default to "Post Name." This will change the structure of the URL's from default (site.com/?p=114 for example) to a good, SEO friendly version (site.com/title-of-post-goes-here).

Now replace the default theme with another one, simply find a new theme that is simple and "clean" - use the automated theme installation process from within Wordpress.

"Appearance" then "Themes" (while logged into Wordpress) then click the "Install Themes" tab. Leave all of the fields empty (they are by default) and then click the "Find Themes" button.

Next, Clean the theme from unnecessary elements - by default, most themes have the sidebar loaded up with useless things like META links, a calendar, archives etc. The footer also typically contains one or more links that can be removed and there are a few other useless things included by default as well. So the next step is to clean all of that up! We don't want excessive external links draining the authority we generate, which could be going back into our internal pages. And we want everything focused on the content and the ads.

Now you need to set the homepage to show only one article - it needs to look more like a static site and less like a blog. Primarily because it reduces canonical URL's and duplicate content. To do this, you're going to publish the homepage article as a page rather than as a post!

Once you've done that, click "Settings" then "Reading" and select the "A static page" radio button and then next to "Front page" select the page that is optimize for your keyword and then click "Save Changes." Now view your site in a browser and you should see that article, and that article only, on the homepage.

Now Clean up the footer and the sidebar and remove any unneeded links like the link to the theme creator's website, the link to Wordpress, Etc.

What theme should you choose for your Wordpress site?

While there are many free Wordpress themes out there, I recommend you use a theme called Thesis (If the link doesn't work, copy and paste the following URL into a browser: **http://www.liraz.com/thesis**). This is much more than a theme, it's more of a design and template manager for Wordpress and it's the best theme for a business site that is meant to be ranked high on the search engines.

Now what about content?

You need to start with at list 6 article pages for a new site. Each article should be 500 to 1000 words long.

The best source for site content is a service called Article Builder (If the link doesn't work, copy and paste the following URL into a browser: **www.liraz.com/articlebuilder**).

Article Builder produces high quality unique articles built around the topics and keywords that you give it. Each article is built by weaving together snippets to build an article based on your category and subtopic choices. They have tens of thousands of categorized snippets in the database, every time you generate an article, it's different!

If article builder does not have articles in your topic you'll have to contract someone to write the articles for you, this is not expensive. Simply run a Google search for "article writing" or "articles writers" and you'll get plenty of offers.

In addition to being a good source of content Article Builder has another extremely useful feature. It can post content automatically to your Wordpress site on the schedule you choose. Why this is important? because Google likes sites that are being updated with new material on a regular basis. It is recommended that you set Article Builder to post a new article to your site once a week or about 3 articles monthly, this way you'll gain some extra points with Google.

Now here is a trick to creating articles fast and cheap. This is not very ethical and I am a bit shame telling you I did it, but anyway since I pledged to tell you all my tricks (or at least most of them ;-), I fill obliged to tell you about this one too, just that you'll know that this is available.

Here's how it works, you run a Google search with your topic as the search term, you add the word 'tips' or 'Guide' to the search. Now you collect several snippets from different good on topic articles that came in the search. next, you combine these snippets into one article. Now you spin this article with a spinner software to get an entirely new article. Just make sure you use the manual spinning mode so that your article will make sense.

In case you are not familiar with the concept of "spinning articles" here are some explanations. With this process you utilize a simple software program that takes an original article and alter it using replacement words (synonyms via an automated thesaurus) in order to create entirely new articles without having to re-write them. It's called "spinning" an article. This have many uses in the Internet Marketing field and we will talk about it later when we discuss linking strategies.

The best spinner software on the market today is called... The Best spinner (If the link doesn't work, copy and paste the following URL into a browser: **www.liraz.com/bestspiner**). If you wish to be a successful internet marketer you need to familiarize yourself with this concept. They have on their site a nice video explaining its uses. You should take a look.

Optimizing Your Site For the Search Engines

Once you have your pages and content in place it's time to

optimize them so that your pages will rank as higher as possible on Google and the other search engines. In this section we'll deal with the "On Page" optimization.

While the "Off-Page" optimization, mainly the external linking structure (that we'll discuses later), is what will give you your unfair advantage - the on-page optimization is a pre-requisite for the off-page to succeed. What I mean to say is that if the on-page optimization is not done right, the best off-line optimization in the world will not help you one bit. so you need to pay attention here.

I'll walk you now step by step in what you need to do:

1. Title tag - this is an HTML tag that goes within the header section of the page. Title tags are the most important on-page factor for SEO. Your keyword should be included within the title tag preferably close to the beginning of it. This is what Google shows on its search results page so you should also make it attractive so that it will entice searchers to click on it. Don't just throw your keyword there, make sure that it is appealing.

2. Headline tags (H1, H2, H3) - make sure your page include one H1 tag with your keyword in it. This headline tag shows Google that the text within it is important to the intended audience.

3. Meta Description tag - while this does not have a bearing on the ranking of the page, Google still pulls the text of how it describes your page to other people from this tag - be sure to make it attractive so that more people will be clicking your page.

4. Images - you should include at list 2 images in each page. Also add one video to one of the pages in your site, you can simply embed a video from YouTube. Make sure one of the images has your keyword in its ALT tag. All other images need to also have ALT tags but should not include your keyword in them. Too many ALT tags with your keyword can lead to an over optimization penalty by Google.

4. Keyword density - the exact keyword density is not important, I'll say it again, the exact percentage of the keyword density is not import. Simply include about 3 instances of your keyword in each page, one of them should be close to the beginning of the article, one of them can be in Bold or Italics and that will do (do not be tempted to overdo it - that's a common newbie mistake).

5. Synonyms - you can include 2 or 3 synonyms to your page that does not include exact words from your keyword.

6. Article Topic - this is important- your content should be on topic and match the niche and the keyword that is being targeted.

7. Outbound link - add one outbound link pointing to an authority site in your topic. This could be a Wikipedia page in a similar topic to yours. Place it at the bottom of the page, you can call it 'recommended source' or something similar. Ah, and do not add a 'no follow' tag to it, leave it in a natural state.

8. Unique Content - the page should be unique and not a duplicated one, if you are using a spun article it should be at least 75% unique. it should also be making sense and has decent grammar.

9. Length of articles - each page should be between 500 and 1000 words long. Be sure to vary the length of the articles in a site. Don't make all the articles exactly the same size.

Once your site is online and the on-page optimization is set, it's time to start creating links pointing to it. That's the subject of our next chapter.

6. Effective Link Building Strategies

Search rankings for a specific keyword are primarily driven by the backlinks to your website using that keyword in the anchor text. But not all backlinks are treated equally. The more powerful a back link is, the more "juice" it flows into your website. And the more "link juice" that flows into your website, the higher your website ranks in search results. So both quantity and quality of back links are important in ranking higher in search results.

Getting external links, the link building phase of the Amazing Formula is the single most critical factor for attaining high rankings and consequently making money online.

Your link building activities are what will make or break your online business. On one hand, when done right, it can blast your pages to the top of Google - on the other hand, even a small mistake can drop your pages into the Google abyss.

Too many links containing the exact same anchor text - Boom, Busted!

Too many links from low quality sites - Boom, Busted!

Too many links coming from just one genre (e.g. only from directories) - Boom, Busted!

Too many links coming from non relevant pages - Boom, Busted!

You get the picture...

That is why I strongly encourage you to acquire every piece of link building knowledge you can lay your hands on. Sorry pal, there is no way around it. if you wish to succeed in internet marketing you must know link building. Even if you are planning to outsource your link building tasks, you should be able to supervise everything that is done for you, and you should ask that they get your approval in advance for all the details of each linking campaign they run for you.

Listen to what happened to me once...

One of my sites had a page that was ranked #6 on the first page of Google's search results for a very competitive term for a couple of years. This page was earning me a nice sum of money day in and day out. One day I decided to try to improve its ranking, I contracted a firm from the Philippines to do a small manual linking campaign for this page. This firm came highly appraised on the forums and the people there were nice and seem knowledgeable. At that time I was busy with a big project and also a bit out of laziness I neglected to ask for a preapproval. To make a long story short, one month and 400 Dollars later my page sank to the fourth page of the Google SERPs.

Now there are two morals to the story:

First, don't count on anyone to do a link building job for you without your approval, in advance, of any small detail of it.

Second, If you have a money producing page ranked anywhere on the first page of Google - don't mess with it!

If you are curious as to what went wrong with this campaign. In the postmortem I discovered that they created too many backlinks with the exact keyword as the link text - and this is something that Google does not like.

Now, the best link building knowledge source that I know of is the Link Building Course (If the link doesn't work, copy and paste the following URL into a browser: **www.liraz.com/linkbuilding**). I strongly encourage you to buy their course. It's a bit pricy but it is well worth the price. Look at it this way, each mistake that is not being avoided due to lack of knowledge can cost you many many times more than the price of this course.

OK, now we are ready to delve into the Amazing Formula's linking strategies.

For our external linking structure we are going to utilize the most effective most powerful linking strategy there is, called "Tiered Linking".

With Tiered Linking you build 3 tiers of links, the links in tier 1 points to your money page, tier 2 points to tier 1 and tier 3 points to tier 2. Basically you are building backlinks to your backlinks. This structure gives your first tier of backlinks more strength and authority. Over time your tier 1 backlinks will gain page rank and that link juice gets passed directly onto your site. It creates a knock on effect passing huge volumes of link juice and authority all the way down the chain to your site. Another advantage of this structure is that it gives search engine spiders thousands of paths and opportunities to land on your site which will further increase rankings.

Here's a diagram that gives you a representation of the Tiered Linking structure:

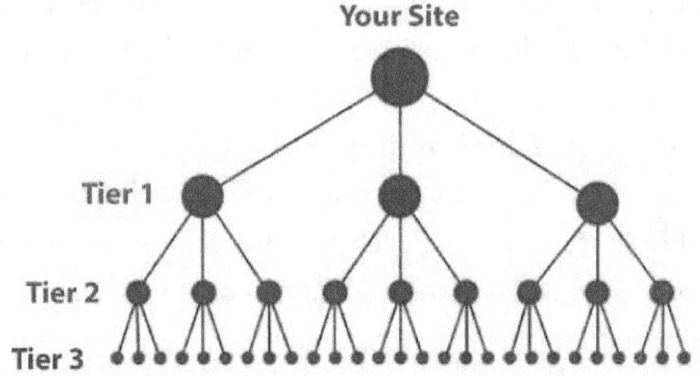

Now let's start with the process of building links for tier 1, these links point directly to your money site.

The links for tier 1 should be created manually and gradually. This means it should be done by you or outsourced to a firm that does manual linking - no automatic software at this phase. It should be spread gradually over two months, faster than that can trigger Google's penalty algos. You can't speed up stuff like building tier 1 links, or else you're going to get penalized.

If you don't have the time or the inclination to do the manual link building yourself, you can outsource it. This is what I'm doing. Manual link building is a tedious task so I usually hire someone else to do it for me. A good and reliable manual link building service that you can hire is Rank Crew (If the link doesn't work, copy and paste the following URL into a browser: **www.liraz.com/rankcrew**). I highly recommend them.

While building tier 1 you need to vary the anchor text as much as possible since Google discount too many instances of exact match anchor text. Follow these guidelines for the link text (anchor text) of your back links:

20% Main keyword exact match (e.g.: "main keyword")

20% Variation of main keyword (e.g.: "best main keyword resource")

50% Generic anchor text (e.g.: "click here, here, clicking here, good resource, see this, have a look")

10% URL of the page as the link text (e.g.: "www.mainkeword.com" or "mainkeword.com" or "http//:www.mainkeword.com")

Now to the actual link building. I can't teach you here all the aspects of doing basic linking, this is beyond the scope of this guide. You should be able to find plenty of resources for that online, or better off, buy the Link Building Course (If the link doesn't work, copy and paste the following URL into a browser: **www.liraz.com/linkbuilding**), this is the best resource of linking knowledge that I know of.

I will however give you some basic guidelines, point you to

the right directions and provide you with a list of sites that can feature links pointing to your site.

Important Note: before you create backlinks with any site, make sure they are not adding the NoFollow tag to their links - do not create tier 1 links with sites that NoFollow their links.

Now here's a list of site's categories where you should build links for your tier 1 (find more sites in the Appendix):

Web 2.0's - great for creating mini sites with articles and videos that link back to your main site. You can use spun articles for the content. Here's where The Best spinner (If the link doesn't work, copy and paste the following URL into a browser: **www.liraz.com/bestspiner**) will come handy. You can use articles that are spun to 50%. Create 10 blogs here and post to them with your link embedded. Make sure the topics are relevant to your keywords, this is important.

Here's a sample of sites in this category (find more in the appendix):
wordpress.com
blogger.com
issuu.com
yola.com
tumblr.com
weebly.com
my.opera.com
livejournal.com

typepad.com
sfgate.com

Social Bookmarking - get your site bookmarked! 30 bookmarks will do it.

Here's a sample of sites in this category (find more in the appendix):
connotea.org
delicious.com
digg.com
reddit.com
slashdot.org
stumbleupon.com
citeulike.org
chime.in
bibsonomy.org
blinklist.com

Directories - web directories are a great source for links - strive for about 40 quality directory links submissions. Seems tedious? there is an excellent tool that can help you with this task. It will make creating manual links from directories a breath. I strongly recommend that you use it: DeepLinkerPro (If the link doesn't work, copy and paste the following URL into a browser: **www.liraz.com/deeplinker**) It allows you to use varied anchor text and also to drip feed the submissions over time to make it all look as natural as possible.

Here's a sample of sites in this category (find more in the

appendix):
wordpress.org/showcase
abc-directory.com
cssdrive.com
cuedirectory.com
dirbull.com
dirnext.com
Elecdir.com
elsf.org
envirolink.org
freeprwebdirectory.com

Blog Directories - If you have a blog get it listed on these sites.

Here's a sample of sites in this category (find more in the appendix):
technorati.com
alltop.com
blogs.com
globeofblogs.com
blogcatalog.com
topix.net/dir
blogtopsites.com
blogtoplist.com
ontoplist.com
hotvsnot.com

Quality Article Directories - You can use spun articles for submission to these directories. Note that the better directories will review your articles before accepting to their site, so make sure they are grammatically correct and make sense. Submit to 30 directories here.

Here's a sample of sites in this category (find more in the appendix):
TheFreeLibrary.com
Ezinearticles.com
GoArticles.com
SelfGrowth.com
Gather.com
ArticlesBase.com
ArticleDashboard.com
ArticleSnatch.com
ArticleCity.com
Isnare.com

Video - create some videos and submit to video sites. You can find at fiverr.com folks that will create a nice video for you for 5 bucks a piece. 3 or 4 video submissions will do for this category.

Here's a sample of sites in this category (find more in the appendix):
youtube.com
vimeo.com
dailymotion.com
metacafe.com
truveo.com
videoegg.com
videobomb.com
veoh.com

liveleak.com
ifilm.com

RSS Directories - Create a RSS feed and submit to these sites. Submit to 30 directories here.

Here's a sample of sites in this category (find more in the appendix):
topix.net
blogdigger.com
feedage.com
feedcat.net
finance-investing.com
jordomedia.com
medworm.com
redtram.com
rssmountain.com
swoogle.umbc.edu

Doc Sharing - Submit a PDF file or a PowerPoint presentation here.

Here's a sample of sites in this category (find more in the appendix):
issuu.com
slideshare.net
scribd.com
docstoc.com
thinkfree.com
keepandshare.com
memoware.com

yudu.com
ziddu.com
docs.zoho.com

Press Releases - a good source for backlinks and news coverage - most of them cost money though.

Here's a sample of sites in this category (find more in the appendix):
businesswire.com
prlog.org
betanews.com
i-newswire.com
pitchengine.com
pr-inside.com
prlog.org
businessportal24.com
cgidir.com
free-press-release.com
information-online.com

Blog Guest Posting - guest blogging is a powerful link building strategy, however, it's a time-consuming pain in the butt! This can boost your rankings but it is not mandatory to the Amazing Formula.

Link Favors - ask friends, Acquaintances and family to place links pointing from their sites to yours.

Creating links for tier 2 and tier 3

Once you have all your tier 1 links set it is time to start

building your tier 2 and tier 3 links.

While with tier 1 we were careful to create our links manually in order for them to appear as "naturally" as possible, with tiers 2 and 3 we can let the quality slip a bit and increase the overall quantity of links that we build.

We still want our links to be contextual and relevant, but we can now use auto generated content on a second tier without a problem. We can worry a lot less about the overall authority and page rank of the domains we are building links from as we start to move the focus away from quality and towards quantity.

For tiers 2 and 3 we are going to leave the "manual" path and move to the "automatic" path. We are going to use a tool that will generate all our tiers 2 and 3 automatically. The best tool for this task is Senuke (If the link doesn't work, copy and paste the following URL into a browser: www.liraz.com/senuke). This is the tool that most successful Internet marketers use.

Senuke is a very powerful backlinking tool which has been designed to assist with the time consuming task of creating a large number of links. I'm not going to describe here how Senuke works as they have videos on their site that describe it better than me. What I can tell you is that with Senuke you can create tired link structures. As much as Senuke is powerful it is very easy to operate, creating tiered links is as easy as moving images on a screen - you need to see it to believe, just go to their site and watch the video. Now, what you do with Senuke is create a 2 tiered structure. It looks like a pyramid - one tier points to another tire that points to one of your tier 1 links - you need to build a different structure for each of your tier 1 links. Use their schedule feature to spread it over time.

Some say that it is safe to also use Senuke for creating the tier 1 links. They may be right, however being the cautious guy that I am, I am not yet ready to test this Hypothesis. I would stick with using only manual methods for the tier 1 links and I strongly advise you to do the same..

In addition to Senuke The Amazing Formula calls for the use of yet another powerful tool called Backlink Booster (If the link doesn't work, copy and paste the following URL into a browser: **www.liraz.com/backlinkbooster**). Backlink Booster automatically increases the power of the backlinks to your website. It's both a backlink indexer aiming to get your backlinks indexed faster, and also a backlink booster to help boost the amount of link juice each of your backlinks sends to your website (use it on your tier 1 backlinks).

Now, if we have Senuke why would we also need Backlink Booster? The fact is that many of the backlinks you are building are never found by Google thus seriously diminishing your linking efforts. What Backlink Booster does is it builds backlinks to your backlinks in a way that all of those backlinks that Google didn't find, are now found by Google. This not just help Google discover all of your backlinks, it also "boost" them so that now more link juice gets passed to your site thus the authority they all possess is multiplied, which flows through to your website! So the end result is more, stronger backlinks!

My tests show that operating Backlink Booster in addition to Senuke creates a strong synergetic effect that translates in a much better Google rankings. It's the one-two punch that will get you that elusive Unfair Advantage. Anyway, in order to rip the full power of the Amazing Formula you need to activate both Senuke and Backlink Booster.

This concludes The blueprint of my success formula for making money online. Once you completed to create tire 2 and 3 links with Senuke and have Backlink Booster do its thing, all you have to do is sit back and watch your site climb the search engines rankings and the money that is pouring into your bank account.

Here's To Your Success

Meir Liraz

# # # #

INTERNET BUSINESS SUCCESS FORMULA

Appendix 1: The 50 Best Paying Affiliate Marketing Markets

The following are the best paying affiliate marketing markets:

Acne
Aging
Allergies
Anxiety
Arthritis
Asthma
Auto Insurance
Back Pain
Beauty
Cancer
Cats
Cosmetic Surgery
Credit Cards
Credit Repair
Debt Consolidation
Depression
Diabetes
Dogs
Email Marketing
Employment
Fitness
Forex
Hair Care
Hair Loss
Health Insurance
Home Improvement
Home Mortgages
Home Owner's Insurance
Home Security
Homeschooling
Insomnia

Internet Marketing
Life Insurance
Muscle Building
Network Marketing
Nutrition
Online casinos
Online Poker
Parenting
Payday Loans
Personal Bankruptcy
Personal Development
Personal Finance
Pregnancy
Quit Smoking
Real Estate
Skin Care
Snoring
Stock Market
Stress
Teeth Whitening
Travel
Web Hosting
Weddings
Weight Loss

INTERNET BUSINESS SUCCESS FORMULA

Appendix 2: Sources for Backlinks Sorted by Category and Page Rank

This list include the following categories:

* Web 2.0's

* Bookmarks

* Directories

* Blog Directories

* Quality Article Directories

* Video

* RSS

* Doc Sharing

* Press Releases

Important Note: before you create backlinks with any of the sites on the following list make sure they are not adding the NoFollow tag to their links - do not create tier 1 links with sites that NoFollow their links.

Web 2.0's

Domain	PR
wordpress.com	9
blogger.com	9
issuu.com	9
yola.com	8

tumblr.com	8
weebly.com	8
my.opera.com	8
livejournal.com	8
typepad.com	8
sfgate.com	8
cerncourier.com	8
angelfire.com	7
tripod.com	7
jimdo.com	7
webnode.com	7
posterous.com	7
over-blog.com	7
webs.com	7
diigo.com	7
bravenet.com	7
newsvine.com	7
squidoo.com	7
jugem.jp	7

INTERNET BUSINESS SUCCESS FORMULA

tripod.lycos.com	7
salon.com	7
goodreads.com	7
alternet.org	7
rediff.com	7
multiply.com	7
plinky.com	7
officelive.com	7
bravejournal.com	7
schuelerprofile.de	7
freewha.com	7
blog.co.uk	6
blogs.rediff.com	6
moonfruit.com	6
zimbio.com	6
fc2.com	6
flavors.me	6
wetpaint.com	6
hubpages.com	6

shutterfly.com	6
quizilla.teennick.com	6
webstarts.com	6
xanga.com	6
podbean.com	6
ucoz.com	6
purevolume.com	6
metafilter.com	6
dailystrength.org	6
democratandchronicle.com	6
wikia.com	6
gather.com	6
skyrock.com	6
carbonmade.com	6
en.netlog.com	6
cafemom.com	6
glogster.com	6
travelblog.org	6
jigsy.com	6

tribe.net	6
blog.de	6
travellerspoint.com	6
zooomr.com	6
piczo.com	6
jazztimes.com	6
dmusic.com	6
fotki.com	6
blogsome.com	6
freeblog.hu	6
twoday.net	6
areavoices.com	6
journalspace.com	6
diaryland.com	6
siteforum.com	6
blinkweb.com	5
doomby.com	5
blogbaker.com	5
http://blogetery.com	5

blogdrive.com	5
onsugar.com	5
opendiary.com	5
thoughts.com	5
ourmedia.org	5
snappages.com	5
spruz.com	5
soup.io	5
sosblog.com	5
dinstudio.com	5
terapad.com	5
webspawner.com	5
migente.com	5
jukeboxalive.com	5
flixya.com	5
ourstage.com	5
sosblogs.com	5
kaneva.com	5
weblogs.us	5

INTERNET BUSINESS SUCCESS FORMULA

hazblog.com	5
ziki.com	5
pinkbike.com	5
yousaytoo.com	5
wayn.com	5
freehostia.com	5
simplesite.com	5
insanejournal.com	5
blogtext.org	5
myanimelist.net	5
webgarden.com	5
blog.hr	5
boulderweekly.com	5
madville.com	5
beep.com	5
springnote.com	5
zoomshare.com	5
scrapbook.com	5
realbuzz.com	5

ewebsite.com	5
fixya.com	5
350.com	5
blogdetik.com	5
quietwrite.com	5
ourstory.com	5
blogetery.com	5
blog.com.es	5
lifeyo.com	5
weblog.ro	5
postbit.com	5
mytripjournal.com	5
galtime.com	5
freeflux.net	5
blogs.ie	5
worldofminecraft.com	5
foss4lib.org	5
busythumbs.com	4
blogskinny.com	4

mywapblog.com	4
mylivepage.com	4
foodbuzz.com	4
wists.com	4
blurty.com	4
wallinside.com	4
vilago21.com	4
nexopia.com	4
bloghi.com	4
getjealous.com	4
lagbook.com	4
supernova.com	4
hpage.com	4
ohlog.com	4
quechup.com	4
inube.com	4
fotopages.com	4
kiwibox.com	4
upsaid.com	4

weddingwindow.com	4
nearlyweds.com	4
spi-blog.com	4
xomba.com	4
tblog.com	4
tabulas.com	4
2itb.com	4
mahiram.com	4
meemi.com	4
profileheaven.com	4
shoutpost.com	4
blogspot.com.au	4
ontheroad.to	4
blog.ca	4
visualsociety.com	4
nireblog.com	4
blogreaction.com	4
pnn.com	4
freeblogspot.org	4

blogeasy.com	4
blogstudio.com	4
bloggum.com	4
bloggerteam.com	4
wikyblog.com	4
freeblogit.com	4
iseekblog.com	4
free-conversant.com	4
singledad.com	4
typolis.net	4
wikipages.com	4
buzzherd.com	3
publr.com	3
bloguni.com	3
iamsport.org	3
incompany.com	3
bizeso.com	3
flippingpad.com	3
sweetcircles.com	3

myindospace.com	3
weblogplaza.com	3
spyuser.com	3
modwedding.com	3
fotolode.com	3
blogge.rs	3
wedshare.com	3
blogono.com	3
iblog.at	3
journalfen.net	3
metsbook.com	3
salsahook.com	3
getwed.com	3
schuelerchat.net	3
blogster.com	2
directorise.com	2
glbsocial.net	2
uwcblog.com	2
medicalmarijuanalisting.org	2

INTERNET BUSINESS SUCCESS FORMULA

siterun.eu	2
gonegothic.com	2
blogpico.com	2
evood.com	2
donkbook.com	2
jacso.hk	2
makinitmag.com	2
inlocaltv.com	1
cloodles.com	1
my.telegraph.co.uk	0
livelogcity.com	0
flukiest.com	0
nyc.net.au	0
yapperz.com	0
deinekollegen.de	0
wheretogetengaged.com	0
hipero.com	0
yolasite.com	0
blogspirit.com	0

blogion.com	0
mynewblog.com	0
20six.co.uk	0
myblogsite.com	0
qapacity.com	0
blogstream.com	0
petbam.com	0
jamrie.com	0
honmag.com	0
jamendo.net	0
blog2blog.nl	0
journalhub.com	0
netcipia.com	0
getjelous.com	0
lastbyte.com	0
kambase.com	0
englandbd.co.uk	0

Bookmarks

<u>Domains</u>	<u>PR</u>

INTERNET BUSINESS SUCCESS FORMULA

connotea.org	8
delicious.com	8
digg.com	8
reddit.com	8
slashdot.org	8
stumbleupon.com	8
citeulike.org	8
chime.in	8
bibsonomy.org	7
blinklist.com	7
diigo.com	7
folkd.com	7
mister-wong.com	7
news.ycombinator.com	7
newsvine.com	7
bizsugar.com	6
jumptags.com	6
tagza.com	6
xmarks.com	6

kaboodle.com	6
tagza.com	6
amplify.com	5
dotnetkicks.com	5
fwisp.com	5
ikeepbookmarks.com	5
kirtsy.com	5
netvouz.com	5
stumpedia.com	5
buddymarks.com	5
clipclip.org	5
dropjack.com	5
linkagogo.com	5
wirefan.com	5
mylinkvault.com	4
oyax.com	4
bookmarktracker.com	4
chipmark.com	4
cloudytags.com	4

de.lirio.us	4
freelink.org	4
bmaccess.net	3
blogbookmark.com	3
rambhai.com	3
blurpalicious.com	0
pineapple.io	0
startaid.com	0

Directories

Domains	PR
wordpress.org/showcase	8
abc-directory.com	7
cssdrive.com	7
cuedirectory.com	7
dir.yahoo.com	7
dirbull.com	7
dirnext.com	7
Dmoz.org	7
Elecdir.com	7

elsf.org	7
envirolink.org	7
freeprwebdirectory.com	7
ilovelanguages.com	7
medranks.com	7
musicmoz.org	7
nutch.org	7
paleoportal.org	7
realtor.com	7
relapi.org	7
thomasnet.com	7
archivd.com	6
art.net	6
bestwebgallery.com	6
Botw.org	6
business.com	6
charitychoice.co.uk	6
cssbased.com	6
cssbeauty.com	6

csselite.com	6
cssheaven.com	6
cssmayo.com	6
dexigner.com/directory/	6
diolead.com	6
directory.ac	6
ehef-newdelhi.org	6
ezilon.com	6
familyfriendlysites.com	6
Fishlinkcentral.com	6
hotvsnot.com	6
intellisparx.org	6
jayde.com	6
jhucr.org	6
joeant.com	6
kahuki.com	6
kinderstart.com	6
mavensearch.com	6
mobileawesomeness.com	6

nzs.com	6
scrubtheweb.com	6
siteinspire.com	6
sitepromotiondirectory.com	6
smsweb.org	6
somuch.com	6
styleboost.com	6
sumodirectory.com	6
thebestdesigns.com	6
ukinternetdirectory.net	6
usacitylink.com	6
vrg.org/links/	6
webdesigners-directory.com	6
webdesignfinders.net	6
webdirectory.com	6
2yi.net	5
aaaagencysearch.com	5
abilogic.com	5
Alivedirectory.com	5

allensguide.com	5
allspiritual.com	5
amphotech.com	5
arakne-links.com	5
artchain.com	5
azoos.com	5
boliviaweb.com	5
britainbusinessdirectory.com	5
britishinformation.com	5
business-directory-uk.co.uk	5
busybits.com	5
canadaone.com/business/	5
canlinks.net	5
capterra.com/browse	5
comeonaussie.com	5
creattica.com	5
css-showcase.com	5
cssleak.com	5
cssnature.org	5

danielmillions.com	5
designflavr.com	5
digmo.org	5
directory-web.net	5
directory.classifieds1000.com	5
directoryworld.net	5
Dirjournal.com	5
dirplanet.in	5
discoverourtown.com	5
divinecss.com	5
dmegs.com	5
domaining.in	5
earthwebdirectory.com	5
elib.org	5
engineersedge.com	5
enquira.com	5
eurobreeder.com	5
exactseek.com	5
Findelio.com	5

INTERNET BUSINESS SUCCESS FORMULA

foliofocus.com	5
frety.net	5
geniusfind.com	5
gimpsy.com	5
globallinknetworks.com	5
gmawebdirectory.com	5
goguides.org	5
healthdirectorymoz.com	5
hotel-base.com	5
html5gallery.com	5
Iillumirate.com	5
incrawler.com	5
iozoo.com	5
itravelnet.com	5
kwika.org	5
lessonplansearch.com	5
linkandthink.org	5
linksgiving.com	5
locanto.com	5

lshmentor.net	5
marketinginternetdirectory.com	5
massivelinks.com	5
mastbusiness.com	5
mastersite.com	5
mundopt.com	5
onemission.com	5
operationuplink.org	5
overlandagency.com	5
rakcha.com	5
re-quest.net	5
resourcelinks.net	5
screenalicious.com	5
screenfluent.com	5
skoobe.biz	5
splashdirectory.com	5
splut.co.uk	5
splut.com	5
submissionwebdirectory.com	5

INTERNET BUSINESS SUCCESS FORMULA

thedesigninspiration.com	5
thetortellini.com	5
traveltourismdirectory.com	5
travelwebdir.com	5
tsection.com	5
ukdirectory.co.uk	5
uncoverthenet.com	5
usalistingdirectory.com	5
volta.net	5
w3csites.com	5
web-design-directory-uk.co.uk	5
web-dir.com	5
websitelaunchpad.com	5
webworldindex.com	5
worldsiteindex.com	5
wv-travel-directory.com	5
zepti.com	5
zorg-directory.com	5
dmegs.com	5

search4i.com	5
101besthtml5sites.com	4
1abc.org	4
247webdirectory.com	4
777media.com	4
9sites.net	4
a1webdirectory.org	4
a1weblinks.net	4
academiamexicanadecine.org	4
alistdirectory.com	4
allworldlinks.com	4
allydirectory.com	4
amidalla.de	4
ananar.com	4
anthonyparsons.com	4
authoritydirectory.com	4
awi-smi.com	4
azlisted.com	4
bestfreewebsites.net	4

INTERNET BUSINESS SUCCESS FORMULA

bizhwy.com	4
blogannounce.info	4
blueboomerang.com	4
brownbook.net	4
buysll.com	4
charitiesdirectory.com	4
charity-charities.org	4
charity.com	4
charitylibrary.co.uk	4
charityportal.org.uk	4
chicagoix.com	4
citystar.com	4
concasida2010.org	4
congoma.org	4
craftdirectory.org/edirectory/	4
craftpop.com	4
craftsitedirectory.com	4
csscount.com	4
cyberwebsearch.com	4

deathndementia.com	4
directory.e-sangha.com	4
directory.v7n.com	4
directory4u.org	4
diroo.org	4
ebjuris.com	4
ethicaldirectory.co.uk	4
expofreightuae.com	4
fasflight.com	4
fedoma.org	4
flookie.net	4
funender.com/free_link_directory	4
gainweb.org	4
gateway-worldwide.com	4
gazingus.org	4
global-weblinks.com	4
gmdir.com	4
goongee.com	4
hedir.com	4

html5-showcase.com	4
html5mania.com	4
humanediteddirectory.net	4
icfmt.org	4
info-listings.com	4
iqnewsroom.com	4
jasminedirectory.com	4
kk-club.com	4
linkaddurl.com	4
linkcentre.com	4
linkopedia.com	4
linkpartnersdirectory.com	4
linkroo.com	4
linksnativos.com	4
linkteve.com	4
macsverige.org	4
mastermoz.com	4
moo-directory.com	4
mygreencorner.com	4

netinsert.com	4
nonar.com	4
ohs.com.au/directory/	4
onlinesociety.org	4
organiclinker.com	4
ozami.com	4
pedsters-planet.co.uk	4
phillyfirstonthefourth.com	4
prolinkdirectory.com	4
puppyurl.com	4
qango.com	4
qualityinternetdirectory.com	4
rdirectory.net	4
rightwingeye.com	4
roask.com	4
saintbarth.org	4
searchsight.com	4
seoseek.net	4
sevenseek.com	4

INTERNET BUSINESS SUCCESS FORMULA

shobby.co.uk	4
siliconsalley.com	4
sites-plus.com	4
slackalice.com	4
spiritsearch.com	4
submitlinkurl.com	4
sundaysalonchicago.com	4
surfsafely.com	4
thalesdirectory.com	4
the-photographer-directory.com	4
tmaonline.net	4
tslindia.org	4
turnpike.net	4
txtlinks.com	4
tygo.com	4
uksuperweb.co.uk	4
unscol.org	4
viesearch.com	4
voxcap.com	4

w3catalog.com	4
web-beacon.com	4
webbozz.com	4
website-services.biz	4
websitespromotiondirectory.com	4
websquash.com	4
welovewp.com	4
wikidweb.com	4
wpbartsdistrict.com	4
wpgala.com	4
wpinspiration.com	4
wwwi.co.uk	4
yoofindit.com	4
zdirectory.net	4
askmatrix.com	4
addurl.nu	4
linkdirectory.com	4
internet-heaven.co.uk/stuff/add.php	4
9ug.com	3

INTERNET BUSINESS SUCCESS FORMULA

alaki.net	3
allstatesusadirectory.com	3
beedirectory.com	3
bigfreeguide.com	3
bigtraveling.com	3
blogaboutmysite.com	3
candydetective.com	3
cssmania.com	3
cwrp.net	3
dearbetty.com	3
devoteclub.com	3
digitaleveuk.org	3
directmylink.com	3
directory.cnjiushang.com	3
directory.pr-club.net	3
directory.ttra2008.com	3
directory.yourartsncrafts.com	3
dirwizard.com	3
divide.org.uk	3

documentosbinarios.com	3
donation4charity.org/pages/charity-directory	3
dreamsubmitting.mylinea.com	3
eicq.org	3
eliteanswers.com/directory/	3
ewilla.com	3
fairelection.us	3
freewebsitedirectories.com	3
gii.in	3
gizmopromo.net	3
goexporters.com	3
gosearchbusiness.com	3
greenstalk.com	3
gzzt.org	3
herlight.com	3
html5elite.com	3
html5websites.net	3
hydeparkbooks.com	3
indexking.net	3

iowasilver.com	3
jaborwhalky.com	3
linknow.co.nz	3
lookforth.com	3
marketingwho.com	3
nadrealizem.com	3
netwerker.com	3
netzoning.com	3
newhealthdirectory.com	3
nkssnet.net	3
nometrix.com	3
onlineshoppers.ca	3
pmarketing.com	3
primodirectory.com	3
reallyfirst.com	3
rubberstamped.org	3
search-o-rama.com	3
searchwebworld.com	3
secondwavesystems.com	3

sitesnoop.com	3
sonoracelticfaire.co	3
speedydirectory.com	3
sudanow.net	3
thebrickwall.com/directory/	3
thegreatdirectory.org	3
ukcharities.org	3
usawebsitesdirectory.com	3
worldwidelist.net	3
wpfloat.com	3
yourjoker.com	3
directory-free.com	2
directory-global.com	2
emedinews.com/directory/	2
html-five.net	2
iwebtool.com/directory/	2
kiwidir.com	2
needaccomodation.com	2
pegasusdirectory.com	2

INTERNET BUSINESS SUCCESS FORMULA

site-sift.com	2
webahead.net	2
websiteopening.com	2
almapubliclibrary.org	0
bigall.com	0
hitwebdirectory.com	0
directoryexpert.org	
rapidenetwork.eu	
douz.org	
webbozz.com	

Blog Directories

Domains	PR
technorati.com	8
alltop.com	7
blogs.com	7
globeofblogs.com	7
blogcatalog.com	6
topix.net/dir	6
blogtopsites.com	6

blogtoplist.com	6
ontoplist.com	6
hotvsnot.com	6
blogs.botw.org	6
blogarama.com	6
blogflux.com/	6
icerocket.com	6
bloggernity.com	6
blogrankings.com	6
bloghub.com	6
blogsrater.com	6
zimbio.com/company/bloggers	5
topblogarea.com	5
bloglisting.net	5
bloghints.com	5
loadedweb.com	5
webworldindex.com	5
addyourblog.com	5
crayon.net	5

INTERNET BUSINESS SUCCESS FORMULA

blogdirs.com	5
bloggernow.com	5
bloggingfusion.com	5
placeblogger.com	5
regator.com	5
blog-directory.org/add-blog.php	5
bloguniverse.com	5
minnesota.com/blog-directory	5
blogville.us	5
nycbloggers.com	5
blog-search.com	5
buzzerhut.com	5
blogscanada.ca	5
delightfulblogs.com	5
blogtree.com	5
blogbal.com	5
bloglinker.com	5
theweblogreview.com	5
flookie.net	5

topofblogs.com	4
blogs.avivadirectory.com	4
rateitall.com/s-4679-blog-directory.aspx	4
blurtit.com	4
theseoking.com	4
fybersearch.com	4
info-listings.com	4
bloggerschoiceawards.com	4
blogio.net	4
A1weblinks.net	4
topsiteswebdirectory.com	4
blogskinny.com	4
blogadr.com	4
feedplex.com	4
feedmap.net	4
wilsdomain.com	4
blogdirectory.net	4
blogdire.com	4
blogsrating.com	4

sarthak.net	4
roask.com	4
blogsitelist.com	4
spillbean.com	4
photarium.com	4
blogpoint.com	4
spicypage.com/	4
blogsbycountry.com	4
blogdirectorysubmission.com	4
blogannounce.info	4
lazyblogdirectory.com	4
blogratings.com	4
top-blogs.org	4
wordpressblogdirectory.com	4
blogdirectory.ws	4
bloguniverse.org	4
webloogle.com	4
goblogz.com	4
blogdirectory.org.uk	4

lisblogsource.net	4
freewebs.com/blogotion	3
portal.eatonweb.com	3
lsblogs.com	3
blogs-collection.com	3
bloggeries.com	3
blogzoop.com	3
blogratedirectory.com	3
search4blogs.com/bloggers/index.php	3
blogsthatfollow.com	3
blogsforsmallbusiness.com	3
blogdir.co.uk	3
blogfolders.com	3
birminghambloggers.contactbox.co.uk	3
bloggerhq.net	3
blogshaven.com	3
websandiego.org/business/reg.php	3
blogwebdirectory.com	3
gozoof.com	3

INTERNET BUSINESS SUCCESS FORMULA

blog.directory-seek.com	3
blogpopular.net	3
conseillemoi.net	3
bloggersdirectory.org	3
blogscollection.com	3
shoutyoursite.com	3
alotofblogs.com	3
boosterblog.net	3
aveblogs.com	3
directoryblogs.com	3
blogirific.com	3
blogpopular.com	3
wutzle.com/browse.php	3
blogsranker.com	3
liquida.com	2
bestblogs.org	2
ablogin.com	2
anse.de	2
blogvillage.gotop100.com	2

directory.bloggertalk.net	2
2searchblogs.com	2
ajdee.com/pages/Blogs/index.html	2
blogicas.com/directory	2
surrealblog.com	2
listablog.com	2
goblog4i.com	2
bloghitlist.com	2
creative-blogs.com	2
problogdirectory.com	2
blogification.com	2
themillionblogs.com	2
freeblogdirectory.info	2
blogdesam.com	2
blogsearchengine.com	1
mylot.com/w/blogs/default.aspx	1
britblog.com	1
fuelmyblog.com	1
blogdirectory.ckalari.com	1

INTERNET BUSINESS SUCCESS FORMULA

bldir.net	1
weblogs.co.in	1
ultimateblogdirectory.com	1
pinoyblogger.com/directory	1
geoblogdirectory.com	1
heliosblogs.com/allcats.html	1
bloggercyber.com	1
bloggerinternet.com	1
exclusivedirectory.net	1
bloggerglobal.com	1
blogswirl.com	1
directories.totalblogdirectory.com	0
blog-collector.com	0
mynewblog.com/lastsites	0
blogdumps.com/index.php	0
blogit.com/blogs/default.aspx	0
blogtagstic.com	0
directory.ubdaily.com	0
splogspot.com (www.)	0

blloggs.com	0
directory.blogaz.net	0
urldigger.com	0
global-blogs.info	0
bloggazines.com	0

Article Directories

Domains	PR
TheFreeLibrary.com	7
Ezinearticles.com	6
GoArticles.com	6
SelfGrowth.com	6
Gather.com	6
ArticlesBase.com	5
ArticleDashboard.com	5
ArticleSnatch.com	5
ArticleCity.com	5
Isnare.com	5
YouSayToo.com	5
Focus.com	5

IdeaMarketers.com	4
SooperArticles.com	4
Amazines.com	4
ArticleRich.com	4
ArticleBlast.com	4
ArticleTrader.com	4
Wrytestuff.com	4
EvanCarmichael.com	4

Video Sharing

youtube.com	9
vimeo.com	9
dailymotion.com	7
metacafe.com	7
truveo.com	7
videoegg.com	7
videobomb.com	7
veoh.com	6
liveleak.com	6
ifilm.com	6

stickam.com	6
stupidvideos.com	6
blinkx.com	6
magnify.net	6
sevenload.com	6
grindtv.com	6
selfcasttv.com	6
flixya.com	5
ourmedia.org	5
mefeedia.com	5
orb.com	5
videosift.com	5
shozu.com/portal	5
pandora.tv	5
eyespot.com	5
vmix.com	5
mediamax.com	5
phanfare.com	5
clipshack.com	5

INTERNET BUSINESS SUCCESS FORMULA

gofish.com	5
freevlog.org	5
loomia.com	5
glidedigital.com	5
vongo.com	5
vlogmap.org	5
dropshots.com	4
bigcontact.com	4
flurl.com	4
bofunk.com	4
fireant.tv	4
broadbandsports.com	4
clipmoon.com	4
gawkk.com	4
vidmax.com	4
sumo.tv	4
qoof.com	4
openvlog.com	4
podesk.com	4

popcast.com	4
tubetorial.com	3
magnoto.com	3
poddater.com	3
pixparty.com	3
grinvi.com	3
pooxi.com	3
divicast.com	3
broadsnatch.com	3
woomu.com	3
everybit.com	3
custom-niche-videos.com	2
evideoshare.com	2
boltfolio.com	2

RSS Directories

Domains	**PR**
topix.net	7
blogdigger.com	6
feedage.com	6

INTERNET BUSINESS SUCCESS FORMULA

feedcat.net	6
finance-investing.com	6
jordomedia.com	6
medworm.com	6
redtram.com	6
rssmountain.com	6
swoogle.umbc.edu	6
automotive-links.mustangv8.com/RSS-directory	5
chordata.info	5
gabbr.com	5
plazoo.com	5
rssmicro.com	5
rsstop10.com	5
urlfanx.com	5
5z5.com	4
educational-feeds.com	4
feedagg.com	4
feedplex.com	4
feedsee.com	4

keegy.com	4
medical-feeds.com	4
newzalert.com	4
ngoid.sourceforge.net	4
oobdoo.com	4
paiddirectory.com	4
political-humor.net	4
postami.com	4
rss-directory.us	4
rssbuffet.com	4
rssmotron.com	4
solarwarp.net	4
4guysfromrolla.aspin.com	3
anatech.net	3
moneyhighstreet.com	3
rsschomp.com	3
rssfeeds.org	3
xmeta.net	3
anse.de/rdfticker	2

feedgy.com	2
goldenfeed.com	2
wingee.com	2
leighrss.com	1
readablog.com	1
feedlisting.com	0
millionrss.com	0
rssfeeds.com	0

Doc Sharing

Domains	PR
issuu.com	9
slideshare.net	8
scribd.com	8
docstoc.com	7
thinkfree.com	7
keepandshare.com	6
memoware.com	6
yudu.com	6
ziddu.com	6

docs.zoho.com	6
slideboom.com	6
authorstream.com	6
edocr.com	5
filefactory.com	5
uploading.com	5
wepapers.com	5
esnips.com	5
my.huddle.net	5
slideserve.com	5
pdfcast.org/pdf/	5
easy-share.com	4
gigasize.com	4
glasscubes.com	4
slingfile.com	4
slidelive.com	4
myplick.com	4
docuter.com	3
doxtop.com	3

INTERNET BUSINESS SUCCESS FORMULA

gazhoo.com	3
kewlshare.com	3
bookgoo.com	3
slideburner.com	3
midupload.com	2
persianupload.net	2
zshare.net	0
gotomyfiles.com	0
twidox.com	0
pex.webexone.com	0
re-pdf.com	

Press Releases

Domains	**PR**
businesswire.com	7
prlog.org	6
betanews.com	6
i-newswire.com	6
pitchengine.com	6
pr-inside.com	6

prlog.org	6
businessportal24.com	5
cgidir.com	5
free-press-release.com	5
information-online.com	5
live-pr.com	5
newswiretoday.com	5
openpr.com	5
prleap.com	5
przoom.com	5
pr.com	5
sbwire.com	5
pressbox.co.uk	4
afly.com	4
bignews.biz	4
businessservicesuk.com	4
clickpress.com	4
dmnnewswire.digitalmedianet.com	4
freepressindex.com	4

INTERNET BUSINESS SUCCESS FORMULA

ideamarketers.com	4
it-analysis.com	4
it-director.com	4
onlineprnews.com	4
prfire.co.uk	4
prfree.com	4
prmac.com	4
pressbox.co.uk	4
pubarticles.com	4
theopenpress.com	4
enewswire.co.uk	4
1888pressrelease.com	4
addpr.com	3
bigrockwebdirectory.com	3
signup.ecommwire.com	3
exactrelease.com	3
express-press-release.net	3
free-press-release-center.info	3
itbsoftware.com	3

mediasyndicate.com	3
newsmakers.co.uk	3
prurgent.com	3
pr9.net	3
pressabout.com	3
pressexposure.com	3
pressmethod.com	3
prfocus.com	3
ukprwire.com	3
usprwire.com	3
postafreepressrelease.com	2
prfriend.com	2
prbd.net	2
pressreleasecirculation.com	2
releasewire.org	2
emeapr.com	1
netforcepress.com	1
astro-business.com	0
bitboot.com	0

INTERNET BUSINESS SUCCESS FORMULA

clickanews.com	0
clickanews.net	0
netbizresources.com	0
netforcenews.com	0
netforcepr.com	0
netforcetechnology.com	0
newsactive.net	0
newsinsites.com	0
newsphase.com	0
our-newsletter.com	0
pagerelease.com	0
pr80.com	0
pressreleasesonline.co.uk	0
seenation.com	0
tectrical.com	0
technifuture.com	0
technofrantic.com	0

MEIR LIRAZ

www.ingramcontent.com/pod-product-compliance
Lightning Source LLC
Chambersburg PA
CBHW070650220526
45466CB00001B/379